To Phil
Love, from Mary, Anne & Abigail

Alexander Sturgis

INTRODUCING
REMBRANDT

Little, Brown and Company

Boston   New York   Toronto   London

First U.S. Edition
Developed and produced by Belitha Press Ltd., 31 Newington Green, London, England N16 9PU, 1994

ISBN 0-316-82022-9
Library of Congress Catalog Card Number 93-11418

10 9 8 7 6 5 4 3 2 1

Published simultaneously in Canada by Little, Brown & Company (Canada) Limited

Printed in Singapore

Title page art: Rembrandt, *Self-Portrait,* 1632.
Contents page art: Rembrandt, Detail from *The Night Watch,* 1642 (see pages 18–19).

Photographic credits

Alte Pinakothek, Munich/Artothek: 4. Bridgeman Art Library: 10/11. British Library: 7 top left. British Museum: front and back cover sketches; title page; 5 top, center, and bottom left; 12/13; 15 right and bottom left; 22 right; 23 left; 24/25, 25, 31. Duke of Sutherland Collection, on loan to the National Gallery of Scotland: 5 top right. Dulwich Picture Gallery: 27 top right. English Heritage: front cover painting. Mary Evans Picture Library: 8. Frankfurt Städelsches Kunstinstitut/Artothek: 16 bottom, 17 bottom. Frans Halsmuseum Haarlem: 14. Graphische Sammlung Albertina, Vienna: 15 top left. Herzog Anton Ulrich-Museum, Braunschweig: 11 top right. The House of Orange Nassau Historic Collections Trust: 9 right. The Hutchison Library: 12 top right. The Louvre/Giraudon: 27 left. Musée Condé/Giraudon: 9 top left. National Gallery, London: 6, 7 bottom right, 16 top, 17 top, 21 bottom, 23 top and center right, 29, 30 bottom left and right. National Gallery of Scotland: 20 right. Residenzgalerie Salzburg: 21 top right. The Rijksmuseum, Amsterdam: contents page, 18/19, 19. The Royal Collection, London: 11 bottom right. Scala: bottom right, 22 left. Staatliche Museen Preussischer Kulturbesitz, Berlin: 20 left, 30 left. Jonathan Stephenson: 28. Stockholm Nationalmuseum: 26.

Contents

Rembrandt by Himself

All these pictures are of the same person. Can you tell what sort of man he was? Can you tell what he did?

The man in all these images is Rembrandt, an artist who lived and worked over three hundred years ago. The pictures are not only of him but they are by him as well.

It is not evident from these portraits that Rembrandt was a painter. He often painted himself in fancy dress or as a rich man-about-town rather than in a painter's apron holding a paintbrush. Perhaps this was because he wanted people to think of him as a wealthy gentleman rather than as a struggling artist.

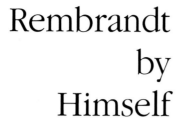

Self-portrait, painting, aged twenty-three, (left).

Self-portrait, etching, aged twenty-four, (right top).

Self-portrait, etching, aged thirty-three, (right bottom).

Self-portrait, etching, aged twenty-four, (right middle).

Rembrandt did not write about his life, but in these pictures he tells us a great deal about himself. Looking at these self-portraits, we can see him growing from a young twenty-three-year-old into an old man of sixty-three. Notice how his self-image changes as he gets older.

After you have read more about Rembrandt, you can look at these portraits again and see if your ideas have changed.

Self-portrait, painting, aged fifty-one, (right).

Self-portrait, painting, aged sixty-three, (below).

Early Years

Rembrandt Harmenszoon van Rijn is one of the few men or women in history recognizable from just his first name. Others are Napoleon, Michelangelo, and Cleopatra. His surname, van Rijn, means "from the Rhine." The Rhine is one of the great rivers of Europe. Rembrandt was born in 1606 at Leiden, Holland, near where the river finally reaches the sea. His father, Harmen, was a miller who owned a windmill outside the city walls that ground malt for making beer.

Rembrandt went to school until he was thirteen, when he left to learn to be a painter. Although this age seems young, most boys at that time left school when they were ten, and most girls did not go to school at all.

Judas Returning the Thirty Pieces of Silver, 1629.
Constantin Huygens saw this painting when he visited the young Rembrandt's studio. He described the figure of Judas as "demented, wailing . . . with an awful face, torn hair, clothes torn to shreds, twisted limbs and hands clenched so hard they bleed."

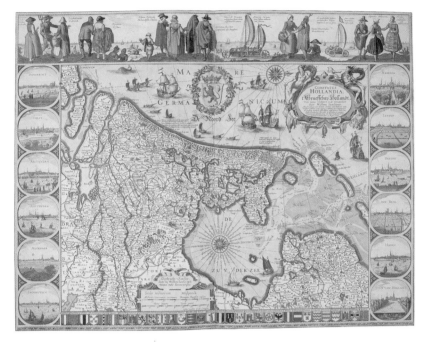

This Dutch map of 1606 shows Rembrandt's birthplace, Leiden. The old map has been drawn at a strange angle. The correct position of the Netherlands is shown above.

Rembrandt started training to be a painter by becoming a painter's apprentice (see illustration on page 14). As an apprentice Rembrandt did all kinds of odd jobs around the artist's studio, such as mixing paints and cleaning brushes, as well as learning to paint. After studying in Leiden for three years, Rembrandt went to finish his training in Amsterdam, now Holland's capital. He studied there for six months with a painter named Pieter Lastman (1583–1633).

Rembrandt was now seventeen, and he returned to his hometown as a fully trained painter. Together with another young painter, Jan Lievens (1607–74), he started his own studio. A visitor to the studio was amazed by the work of the two young artists. "Never have I come across such hard work and dedication," he wrote. The visitor, Constantin Huygens, was an important man himself. He was looking for artists to paint pictures for the palaces of the Dutch leader, Prince Frederick Henry. When he saw Rembrandt's work, he was sure he had found the right man.

Thomas de Keyser, *Constantin Huygens and His Clerk,* 1627. Constantin Huygens was one of the first men to recognize Rembrandt's genius.

Holland in the Seventeenth Century

Before Rembrandt's birth, Belgium, Luxembourg, and Holland were one country, known as the Netherlands. From the early 1500s to 1579, the Netherlands were ruled by the king of Spain, but in this year the country was split in two. The southern part of the country stayed under Spanish rule, and the northern part of the Netherlands — which we now call Holland — broke away to rule itself. The new country was made up of seven of the seventeen provinces (regions or counties) that had made up the Netherlands and was known as the United Provinces or the Dutch Republic. A republic is a country without a king or queen that governs itself. Although there was no king

This map of 1630 shows Europe as it was during Rembrandt's lifetime. The arrow points to Holland.

Jacob van der Ulft, *Dam Square,*
Amsterdam, 1659.
The enormous town hall of Amsterdam
(*left*) was started in 1648 and filled
with paintings and sculpture by the
artists of the city. Rembrandt created a
huge painting for the town hall of which
only a part survives (see pages 26 and 27).

of the Dutch Republic, they did have a leader
called the stadtholder. In Rembrandt's time this
leader was Prince Frederick Henry.

This new country was an exciting place for
painters. Prince Frederick built palaces, which
had to be decorated with paintings. In the cities
the new rulers built town halls, which they also
filled with paintings. But it was not just the rulers
of the Dutch Republic who bought paintings.
Visitors to Holland from England were amazed
by the number of paintings ordinary people had
in their homes. The visitors commented that
they had never seen a country that loved
painting more.

Gerard van Honthorst, *Prince
Frederick Henry,* 1631.
Here, the Dutch leader of Rembrandt's
time is shown wearing armor. One of
his most important tasks was to lead the
Dutch army against the Spanish, from
whom the Dutch won their
independence.

Portraits — Painting People

When Rembrandt was twenty-five, he moved to the city of Amsterdam to continue his work as a painter. He quickly became the leading portrait painter to the rich families of the city. Everybody who was anybody wanted their portrait painted by the young artist, and people begged him to paint them.

Rembrandt painted nonstop and finished at least one picture every two weeks, of which about half were portraits. Looking at the portraits on this page, you might not realize how rich the people in them were. At this time in Holland,

The Anatomy Lesson of Dr. Tulp (1632) was a very important picture in Rembrandt's career. There were no public museums in Rembrandt's time, but this painting was hung in the surgeon's meeting hall, which people visited, so Rembrandt's fame as a portrait painter spread.

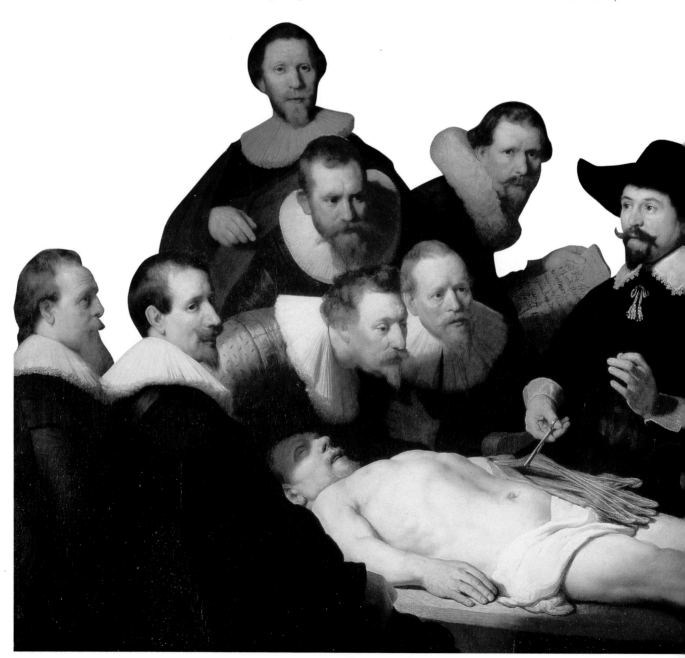

people were worried about showing off their riches and usually dressed in black. But if you look closely, you can see that their clothes are not as simple as they seem. They are made of the finest materials (such as silk, velvet, and lace) and have delicately embroidered patterns on them.

Portraits do not have to picture just one person. *The Anatomy Lesson of Dr. Tulp* (*below left*) is a portrait Rembrandt painted of a group. All these men were members of a society of surgeons (like a club). Rembrandt has not painted them in a row, as in a team photograph, but listening to a lecture given by Dr. Tulp. Dr. Tulp has peeled back the skin of a dead man's arm and is showing his audience the muscles attached to the hand.

We do not know the name of this man (*top right*) or when he was painted, but he was probably an Amsterdam merchant. Oval-shaped portraits were very fashionable at this time, and Rembrandt painted large numbers of them.

Agatha Bas, 1641.
The subject of this portrait belonged to one of Amsterdam's richest families. She wears the finest clothes and is dripping with jewelry. Her thumb sticks out over a painted frame to make us think she is standing at a window.

Amsterdam

When Rembrandt moved to Amsterdam, it was one of the greatest and richest cities in the world. Today, Amsterdam is famous for its canals and flower markets, but at the time, it was the main port in Europe. Ships from Amsterdam sailed all over the world. They collected grain from Russia and traveled as far as America, Japan, and the East and West Indies for more exotic goods such as spices, silk, and tobacco. The goods that came into Amsterdam were sold all over Europe, and the businessmen of the city were in charge of all this trading. In America, New York was settled as a Dutch colony in the early 1600s. New York City was originally named New Amsterdam.

This modern-day photograph of Amsterdam (*left*) shows one of the grand merchant's houses built in Rembrandt's day. In front runs one of the city's many canals.

View of Amsterdam, 1640.
Although he lived in the city for most of his life, Rembrandt made very few pictures of Amsterdam. You can see the windmills for which Holland is still famous. On the left are the masts of the ships that crowded into Amsterdam's harbor.

The merchants of Amsterdam were among the richest in the world. They built themselves grand town houses, which they filled with paintings. It is not surprising that Rembrandt decided to move to the big city.

When Rembrandt arrived in Amsterdam, he joined the studio of Hendrick van Uylenburgh. Hendrick was more of a businessman than a painter. He bought and sold old paintings as well as having new ones painted. Rembrandt soon became his chief painter. Rembrandt would paint the pictures, and Hendrick would sell them. The two men were not just working partners, for in 1634 Rembrandt married Hendrick's cousin Saskia.

Rembrandt the Teacher

This painting, *Artists' Academy* (1656), by the Dutch painter Michiel Sweerts, gives us a good idea of what a drawing class was like in Rembrandt's time. Some of the boys seem to be paying much more attention than others.

Rembrandt's success as a painter meant that young artists wanted to come and learn from him. Even experienced artists who had their own studios came to be taught by the master.

The painting above shows a drawing school during Rembrandt's time. The master, or head, of the studio, in his painter's cap, has his back to us. The young boys draw the semi-nude model, who stands in the middle of the room. Look at the three pictures on the right. The print (*page 15, top right*) is by Rembrandt, but the two drawings are by his students. You can see that they all show the same boy, leaning his elbow on a cushion, but seen from different positions in the room. We can imagine Rembrandt strolling around looking over the shoulders of his students, making comments, while they drew the young boy who is posing.

Rembrandt's students not only learned to draw in his studio, they were also taught how to paint in the master's style. They copied paintings that Rembrandt had made. A visitor to Rembrandt's studio described it as overflowing with his pupils. He also complained that Rembrandt would sometimes add his own signature to paintings done by his students and then sell them as his own.

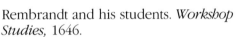

Rembrandt and his students. *Workshop Studies,* 1646.

The drawings at left were made by students in Rembrandt's studio. The print (*below right*) is by Rembrandt and is of the same boy in the same pose. Because prints come out in reverse, it is a mirror image of the drawings. Rembrandt may have made this print and others like it as a model for his pupils to copy and learn from.

Painting Stories

In Rembrandt's time a painter could specialize in different types of painting. Rembrandt was famous for his portraits. Other painters produced landscapes or still lifes. Still lifes are pictures of fruit and flowers or domestic objects.

The kind of painting that was thought to be the most important and difficult was called history painting. This art showed scenes from the Bible (like the two opposite), from Greek or Roman legends, or from history. The painter of stories had to be able to paint people, landscapes (if the stories happened outside), and still lifes as well. Rembrandt's painting *Belshazzar's Feast* (*page 17, top right*) includes two of these elements: figures and a still life of fruit.

Rembrandt's history paintings are very dramatic. He often made them more exciting by creating strong contrasts between light and dark. The paintings look as if they are staged in a theater under a spotlight.

Rembrandt was famous for being able to paint emotions. He did this by painting faces with expression but also by painting bodies in expressive postures. In *Belshazzar's Feast* the king is surprised and frightened. Rembrandt put these feelings into the king's face and body; he looks horrified as he recoils from the hand and its message.

In the painting *The Blinding of Samson* (*page 17, bottom*) it is not fear but anger and agony that Rembrandt wanted to show. Look at Samson's clenched fists and curled toes. These parts of his body tell us how he feels even more than his face does.

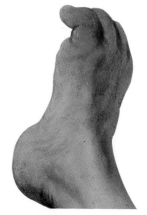

Belshazzar's Feast, c.1635. Belshazzar, the king of Babylon, held a great feast using the silver and gold cups and plates he had stolen from the Temple in Jerusalem. Suddenly a mysterious hand appeared and wrote that the Babylonian kingdom would end soon. That night Belshazzar was killed.

The Blinding of Samson, 1636. Samson was a man with superhuman strength, which came from his long hair. He was tricked by the beautiful Delilah into revealing his secret, and while he was asleep, she cut off his hair. Samson's enemies, the Philistines, then leapt out and captured him. They blinded Samson and imprisoned him.

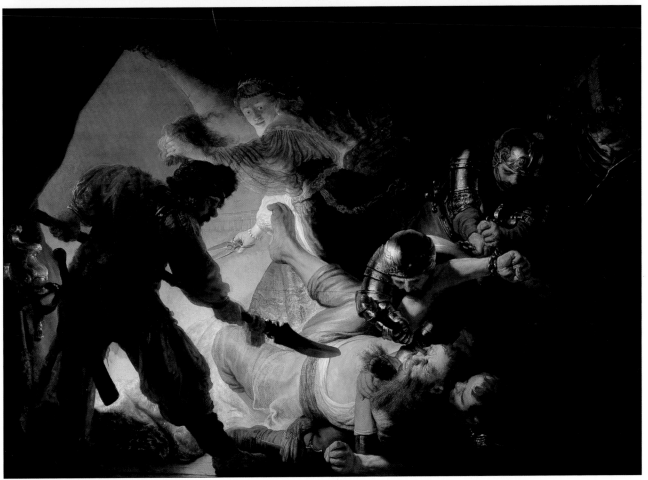

The Night Watch

This is probably Rembrandt's most famous painting. It is known as *The Night Watch*. In fact the title is misleading because the scene is not happening at night — no one has any torches or lanterns — and the people in it are not keeping watch. The picture was first called *The Night Watch* about 150 years after it was painted, probably because it had darkened with age and this made it look as if the scene was happening at night.

Detail from *The Night Watch,* 1642. This is Rembrandt's eye under his painter's beret. He is staring out of the painting at us. Can you find where this detail comes from? He is next to the flag carrier, called the ensign, at the back of the painting.

The photograph (*top right*) gives you an idea of the size of *The Night Watch.*

Although the painting looks as if it might be a scene from a battle, it is actually a group portrait (see pages 10–11). Sixteen of the people in the painting paid to have their portraits included in the picture. Can you figure out which ones they are? The people who were painted at the front would have paid more than those whose faces poke up at the back.

The men in the painting were members of a company of guardsmen. These companies were originally formed to help defend the city, but by Rembrandt's time they had become social clubs for rich townsmen. There were probably about two hundred men in the company, but only the richest could afford to be put into Rembrandt's painting.

The captain of the guardsmen is the man dressed in black with the red sash around his chest. The second-in-command is the man in yellow with the white sash.

Rembrandt's guardsmen do not look posed but as if they are preparing for a battle or a procession. The captain looks as if he is giving a command. Other group portraits of guardsmen look much more posed and unexciting. There is a story that the guardsmen who Rembrandt painted were angered by the painting because it was so unusual. Nonetheless, they paid for it and hung it in their hall, so it seems unlikely that this is true.

Rembrandt and Women

The women in Rembrandt's life frequently appear in his paintings. Sometimes they appear in fancy dress or as a character in a story, or sometimes just as themselves.

The writing on this beautiful drawing at left says that it is of Rembrandt's wife, Saskia, and was drawn three days after they were engaged, when she was twenty-one. There is another picture of Saskia on page 29, where she is dressed as a Roman goddess. But eight years after they were married, Saskia died, leaving Rembrandt with a nine-month-old son called Titus.

After Saskia's death, Rembrandt started a love affair with Titus's nanny, Geertje Dircks. She may be the *Young Woman in Bed* pulling back the curtain to look at something that has caught her eye (*below*).

Rembrandt's young wife, Saskia (*above*), wears a floppy hat and holds a flower. You can see the date of 1633 at the end of the writing underneath the drawing.

Young Woman in Bed, 1645. This young woman may well be Geertje Dircks, whom Rembrandt was to treat so badly. Something has caught the woman's attention and made her pull back the curtain to her bed, but we do not know what it is.

The story of Rembrandt and Geertje is not a happy one. Geertje wanted to marry Rembrandt, but by then he had fallen in love with another woman. Geertje took the painter to court, saying that he had promised to marry her and had broken his promise. The court believed her, and although Rembrandt was not forced to marry her, he did have to pay to support her. Then Rembrandt behaved in a very cruel way. It seems that he helped to have the unfortunate Geertje locked up in a house of correction, a sort of prison, where she stayed for twelve years.

The woman Rembrandt left Geertje for was named Hendrickje Stoffels. Hendrickje never married Rembrandt, which shocked some people at the time, but she lived with him until her death in 1663. Together they had a daughter, Cornelia. The pictures Rembrandt painted of Hendrickje are among his most tender works.

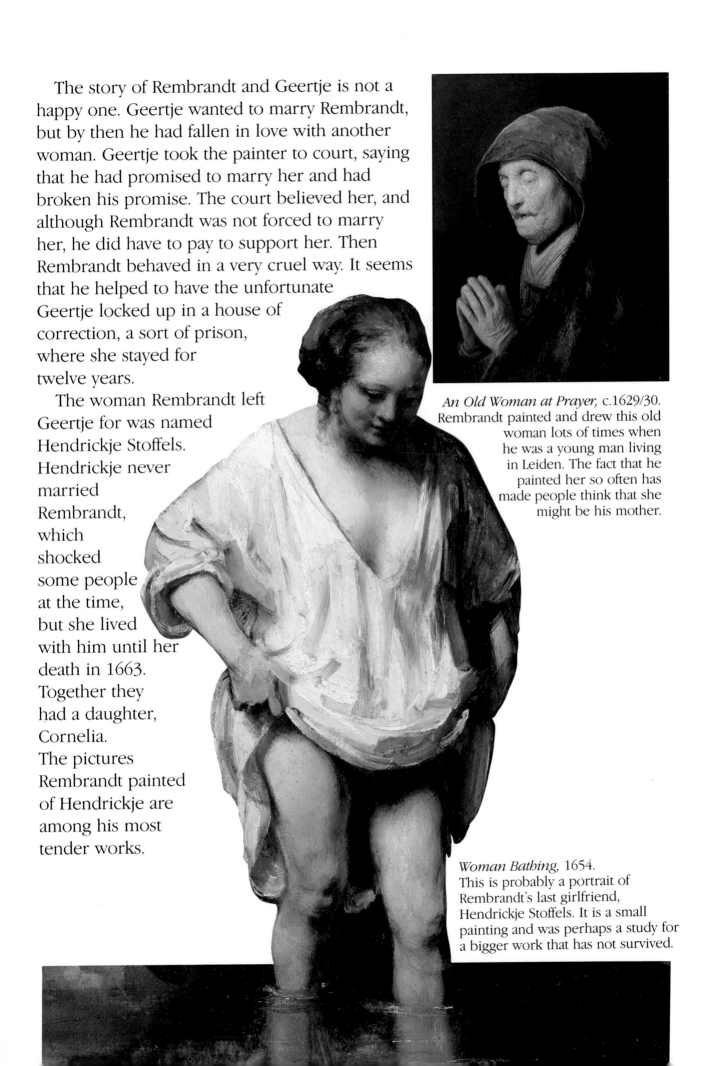

An Old Woman at Prayer, c.1629/30. Rembrandt painted and drew this old woman lots of times when he was a young man living in Leiden. The fact that he painted her so often has made people think that she might be his mother.

Woman Bathing, 1654. This is probably a portrait of Rembrandt's last girlfriend, Hendrickje Stoffels. It is a small painting and was perhaps a study for a bigger work that has not survived.

Painting Bodies

The German artist Albrecht Dürer would have looked at statues like the Roman *Apollo Belvedere* (*below*) when he made this print (*right*), *Adam and Eve* (1504). Because Dürer's work is a print, which comes out reversed, the legs and arms of Adam have come out in reverse of the statue.

On these pages are two prints of Adam and Eve in the Garden of Eden. One is by Rembrandt (*page 23*) and the other (*above*) by an earlier German artist, Albrecht Dürer (1471–1528). Look at the way the two artists have drawn Adam's and Eve's bodies. Which print do you think is more realistic?

When Dürer made his print, he looked at Roman and Greek statues as models for his figures. For Adam, he copied a famous statue of the Roman god Apollo (*left*), and for Eve he looked at statues of the Roman goddess of beauty, Venus. His figures, with their smooth, hard bodies, are more like ancient statues than real people.

Rembrandt's Adam and Eve could not look less like statues. You can see the wrinkles in their skin and their rolls of fat. This shocked some people at the time, who were not used to seeing such realistic pictures of naked people, especially people from the Bible. They thought that artists should try and make the bodies of people they painted look perfectly beautiful, the way classical Greek and Roman statues are. One person writing shortly after Rembrandt had died complained about the flabby flesh and old age of the female bodies in his paintings, saying they looked more like washerwomen than goddesses.

Rembrandt would probably have been pleased with this attack. We know he looked at real people such as his relatives and girlfriends when he painted his pictures.

Detail from *Belshazzar's Feast* (see page 17).

Detail from *Saskia as Flora* (see page 29).

People in Rembrandt's time not only complained about his paintings of naked bodies; some also said that he could not paint hands properly. Here are two hands from paintings that you can see in this book that might make you agree.

The Fall of Man, 1638.
Here is Rembrandt's version of the scene that Dürer had made over one hundred years earlier. As well as making the figures less like statues, Rembrandt has turned the snake into a kind of dragon.

23

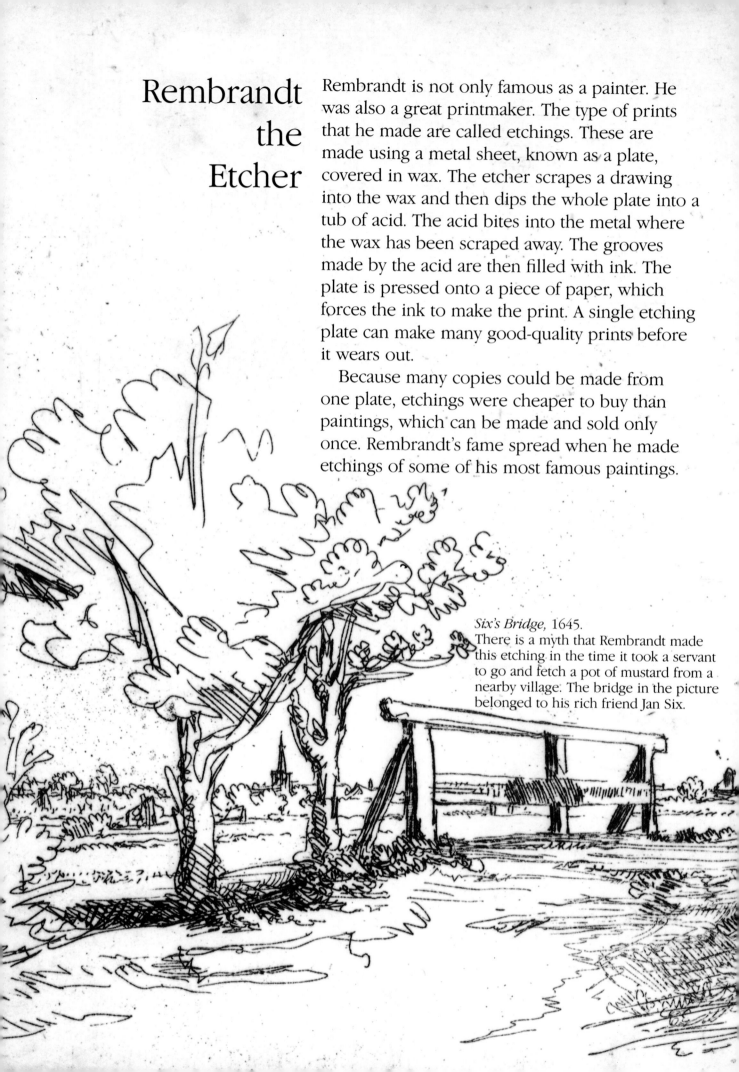

Rembrandt the Etcher

Rembrandt is not only famous as a painter. He was also a great printmaker. The type of prints that he made are called etchings. These are made using a metal sheet, known as a plate, covered in wax. The etcher scrapes a drawing into the wax and then dips the whole plate into a tub of acid. The acid bites into the metal where the wax has been scraped away. The grooves made by the acid are then filled with ink. The plate is pressed onto a piece of paper, which forces the ink to make the print. A single etching plate can make many good-quality prints before it wears out.

Because many copies could be made from one plate, etchings were cheaper to buy than paintings, which can be made and sold only once. Rembrandt's fame spread when he made etchings of some of his most famous paintings.

Six's Bridge, 1645.
There is a myth that Rembrandt made this etching in the time it took a servant to go and fetch a pot of mustard from a nearby village. The bridge in the picture belonged to his rich friend Jan Six.

Rembrandt etched portraits, stories, and subjects that he would not have painted, such as this pig. People would not have bought a grand oil painting of a pig. Rembrandt was always experimenting with his prints.

The Three Crosses, 1653.
These two etchings (*above*) of Jesus on the cross were made from the same etching plate. After making the one on the left, Rembrandt altered the plate. The second etching is much darker. Some figures have disappeared from the foreground, while a man has appeared on a horse in front of the left-hand cross.

Later Life

After the successes of his early life, Rembrandt's old age was full of disappointments and difficulties. Rembrandt seems to have been a difficult man to get along with, and he argued with many of the important people who asked him to paint for them. This meant they often did not ask him a second time.

Today, many people think that Rembrandt's later pictures are his greatest works. But during his old age some people saw his style as old-fashioned and so preferred the paintings of younger artists.

This was not Rembrandt's only problem. When things were going well, Rembrandt spent money as quickly as he earned it. He bought a very expensive house and filled it with a collection of paintings and other art objects. All this was more than Rembrandt could afford, and in 1656 he went bankrupt and had to sell his house and all his possessions.

This is all that remains of Rembrandt's huge painting *The Conspiracy of Julius Civilis* (1661), and even this fragment is over six feet high. In 69 A.D., Julius Civilis, a Dutch nobleman, led a revolt against Roman rule. In this scene, fellow noblemen swear an oath to join his cause.

Near the end of his life he was asked to paint an enormous painting for the new town hall in Amsterdam. Rembrandt must have seen this as a chance to prove himself once more the greatest painter in the city. But the rulers of Amsterdam may have felt that the subjects of the painting were not portrayed with proper nobility. They removed *The Conspiracy of Julius Civilis* from the town hall after only a few months. Today, only part of the painting survives.

The end of Rembrandt's life was a sad one. Both his girlfriend, Hendrickje, and his son, Titus, died before he did, leaving him alone with his young daughter, Cornelia. Rembrandt died on October 4, 1669, at the age of sixty-three.

Portrait of a Young Man, 1668.
This young man is possibly Rembrandt's son, Titus, who died at the age of twenty-seven. Titus learned to be a painter in his father's workshop, but no one knows what his paintings looked like or if they have survived.

Slaughtered Ox, 1655.
This picture was painted the year before Rembrandt was declared bankrupt. It is of an ox's carcass hanging up in a butcher's shop. It is very unlikely that a rich merchant or nobleman asked him to paint a picture of a slaughtered animal.

How Did He Do It?

Brushes in Rembrandt's time were made of pig's bristles tied onto sticks with string. Soft-haired brushes were made from the hairs of stoats and polecats set into pieces of quill from bird's feathers.

The colors Rembrandt used are called earth colors because they are made from different-colored soils ground up with oil.

How did Rembrandt paint the pictures you see in this book? We do not know exactly, but experts have looked long and hard at his paintings to try and discover the secrets of his methods.

Perhaps the best way to discover how Rembrandt painted is to look at one picture in particular. This one is of his wife, Saskia, dressed as the Roman goddess of flowers (*right*). This picture is painted on canvas, but Rembrandt also painted on wood and paper. The paint he used was oil paint, made from ground-up colors mixed with an oil, more like cooking oil than oil for a car. The two main differences between oil paint and paints mixed with water are that oil paints are much thicker and take longer to dry. Rembrandt used these qualities to full effect. He would often put the paint on the canvas in big, thick lumps, sometimes slapping it on with a knife rather than using a brush. If he was painting hair or fur, he would sometimes scrape into the paint when it was still wet with the pointed end of his brush to make a hair-like effect.

Rembrandt did not always use paint in great blobs. If he was trying to paint a canvas to look smooth, like silk or skin, he would put the paint on thinly and evenly. In this way, some of his paintings are almost like sculptures in paint. This is the most difficult thing to see in a book about paintings by Rembrandt. All the pictures look flat and smooth on the page, which is why it is so exciting, and often surprising, to see the originals.

Although this painting of Saskia dressed as the goddess Flora looks flat on the page, you can see from the details the different effects Rembrandt could create with oil paints.

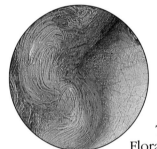

This detail of Flora's hair shows where Rembrandt scratched into the surface of the paint with the pointed handle of his paint-brush. The hair is in contrast to the smooth painting of the skin.

This detail of Flora's belt shows the thick blobs of paint Rembrandt used to create the effect of jewel-encrusted gold.

Did He Do It?

The Man in the Golden Helmet (date unknown), once thought to be one of Rembrandt's greatest works, is now believed to be by one of his students.

The two students of Rembrandt depicted in these self-portraits are Govert Flinck and Carel Fabritius. Both are dressed in ways in which Rembrandt painted himself. Flinck looks so much like his master here that the portrait was thought to be of Rembrandt.

Govert Flinck, *Self-Portrait,* 1633 (*below left*).

Carel Fabritius, *A Young Man with a Feathered Cap,* 1636 (*below right*).

This painting is known as *The Man in the Golden Helmet.* It is one of Rembrandt's most famous works. Look at it carefully. Many of the things we have seen Rembrandt doing in other paintings in this book are here in this painting. It is an expressive portrait. The helmet is painted with thick oil paint, and the artist has used dramatic contrast between light and dark, a technique known as chiaroscuro. Many people have thought that this is one of the greatest paintings in the world.

Everything said above is true except for one thing. Today, experts say that this picture is not by Rembrandt but by one of his students. Look at it again. Has it changed? Of course not, but perhaps the way you look at it has.

Because of Rembrandt's fame and success, many artists tried to copy his style of painting. Rembrandt taught his students to paint exactly as he did. They copied his paintings and then painted their own in his style. Many of Rembrandt's students even dressed like him and painted themselves looking like their master. The paintings below are self-portraits by Rembrandt's students. You can compare them with those by Rembrandt at the beginning of the book.

Some Key Dates

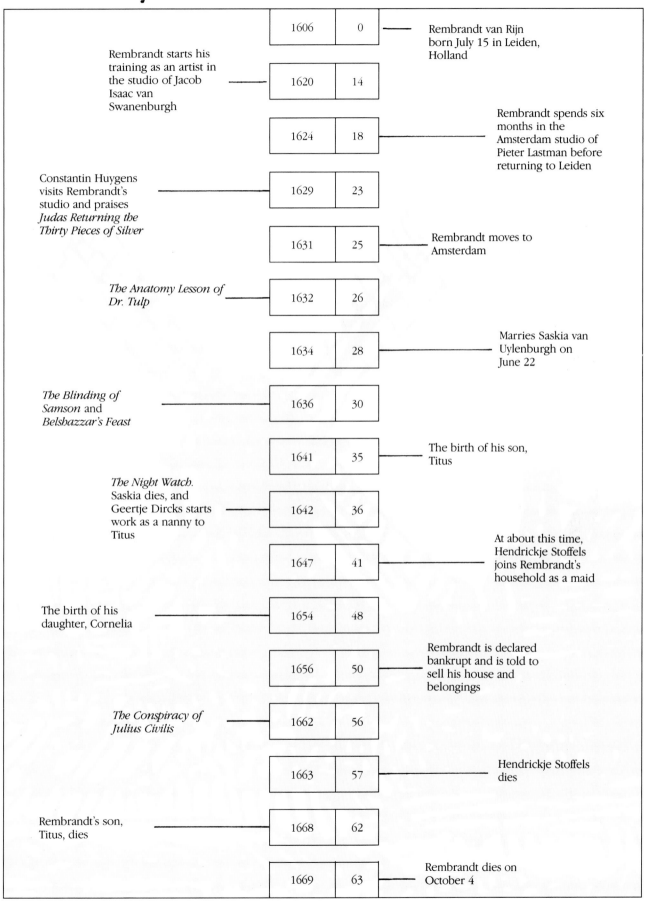

1606	0	— Rembrandt van Rijn born July 15 in Leiden, Holland

Rembrandt starts his training as an artist in the studio of Jacob Isaac van Swanenburgh — | 1620 | 14 |

| 1624 | 18 | — Rembrandt spends six months in the Amsterdam studio of Pieter Lastman before returning to Leiden |

Constantin Huygens visits Rembrandt's studio and praises *Judas Returning the Thirty Pieces of Silver* — | 1629 | 23 |

| 1631 | 25 | — Rembrandt moves to Amsterdam |

The Anatomy Lesson of Dr. Tulp — | 1632 | 26 |

| 1634 | 28 | — Marries Saskia van Uylenburgh on June 22 |

The Blinding of Samson and *Belshazzar's Feast* — | 1636 | 30 |

| 1641 | 35 | — The birth of his son, Titus |

The Night Watch. Saskia dies, and Geertje Dircks starts work as a nanny to Titus — | 1642 | 36 |

| 1647 | 41 | — At about this time, Hendrickje Stoffels joins Rembrandt's household as a maid |

The birth of his daughter, Cornelia — | 1654 | 48 |

| 1656 | 50 | — Rembrandt is declared bankrupt and is told to sell his house and belongings |

The Conspiracy of Julius Civilis — | 1662 | 56 |

| 1663 | 57 | — Hendrickje Stoffels dies |

Rembrandt's son, Titus, dies — | 1668 | 62 |

| 1669 | 63 | — Rembrandt dies on October 4 |

Index

A **bold** number shows the entry is illustrated on that page. The same page often has writing about the entry, too.

Unless otherwise stated, all of the works listed in this index are by Rembrandt.